Communication Skills

A Personal Workshop

Russ Baleson

An environmentally friendly book printed and bound in England by
www.printondemand-worldwide.com

Mixed Sources
Product group from well-managed
forests, and other controlled sources
www.fsc.org Cert no. TT-COC-002641
© 1996 Forest Stewardship Council

FSC

PEFC Certified
This product is
from sustainably
managed forests
and controlled
sources
www.pefc.org

PEFC
PEFC/16-33-415

This book is made entirely of chain-of-custody materials

www.fast-print.net/store.php

COMMUNICATION SKILLS – A PERSONAL WORKSHOP
Copyright © Russ Baleson 2013

Cover Design by Charis Beasley

A catalogue record for this book is available from the British Library

ISBN 978-178035-749-2

First published 2013 by
FASTPRINT PUBLISHING
Peterborough, England.

Contents

Introduction

Russ Baleson is a training expert with over thirty years of professional experience. He is also the author of *'People, Self-Coaching and Management Skills'*.

Best known as a highly effective trainer and coach, he has designed and facilitated numerous skill-building and life-changing workshops in both the United Kingdom and South Africa. His key distinguishable strengths are the passion and skill with which he effects a positive behaviour change in each individual, coupled with his courage to challenge outdated training paradigms.

Russ's Interpersonal and Communication Skills workshops have been attended by thousands of delegates over the years and now he has written the book that so many of them have asked for.

How to use this book

Learning is not complete without putting into practice what you have learned. Reading this book will provide you with many insights and, if you treat it as your own personal workshop and work carefully through the self-reflection and application exercises, it could change your life.

Notebook Exercises

It is highly recommended that you use a notebook to complete the exercises as indicated throughout the book. These exercises have been especially designed to enhance personal awareness, stretch your thinking and aid understanding and retention.

The Aim of this Personal Workshop

The aim of this personal workshop is to build your confidence, knowledge and interpersonal skills in order to maximise your effectiveness in all interactions. It will enable you to:

- Communicate clearly, simply and persuasively in order to build, maintain and nurture relationships with others whilst developing trust and rapport.

- Ensure that in all exchanges, meaningful, ongoing relationships are maintained on a *long-term* basis.

- Motivate and influence people towards mutually beneficial solutions.

- Deal effectively with conflict, complaints and other stressful interactions whilst appropriately managing your own emotions.

- For Managers: Deliver difficult messages and address behavioural issues in a way that motivates and changes behaviour.

Determined by Beliefs and Values

Even though skills can be learned, not everyone can improve their skills by learning them. People learn best and most easily when the skills they are learning are consistent with their beliefs, values and motives. For example, you can't be a good listener if you are not interested in what someone is saying. You will develop your skills much faster by developing your curiosity and learning how to become more interested in others. Questioning too comes from a deep interest and flows naturally from dialogue.

Intention

This book is not a collection of tricks and techniques. If one's intentions are not honourable, all the techniques in the world will not sustain a long-term relationship. Our intentions towards others are determined by our values and beliefs. Our survival has always depended on the quality of our relationships and so we are good at sensing, even on an unconscious level, the underlying intentions of others. Transparency and consistency of behaviour are therefore the keys to creating trust, rapport and developing meaningful relationships.

What Do We Want?

"No one cares how much you know, until they know how much you care."

Theodore Roosevelt

What drives us? What do we want more than anything else from others? We want to be loved. You can imagine the look on my delegates' faces when I tell them that I want them to love me! We all want to belong; feel safe; feel valued; be heard; be seen; be included; be involved; be respected; be listened to; be understood; and be loved. We all want to feel important.

Attention

"Look at me, Dad! Look at me!" You can hear children calling out for attention. You can also see much taller children (adults) calling out for attention by the way they behave and by the things that they say, wear, drive, etc. We feel less alive and less energetic when we do not get enough of this much-needed commodity. For this reason, all the content of this book is centred on Three Key Principles. This is the foundation upon which all the interpersonal skills are built.

Enhance, or at least maintain, the self-esteem of others.

Listen and respond with empathy.

Involve others.

Listening Skills

"There are those that listen, and those who wait to talk."

Paul Williams

Listening Skills

I can't quite remember how I was taught to listen when I was a child but I do remember people saying, *"Just listen to me!"* And other quips like, *"You were given two ears and only one mouth, and therefore you should listen twice as much as you talk."* Were you ever taught how to listen? I've noticed that studying the concept of listening skills has been a first-time experience for most of the adult delegates in my training workshops.

Listening is where all other effective interpersonal skills stem from. Do you find it easy to listen to others? How would your friends and colleagues rate your listening skills?

Notebook Exercise: What Makes It Difficult For You To Listen?

There are many things that make listening in today's fast, active world a challenging task. Ask yourself what makes it difficult for you to listen and list your answers in your notebook before reading any further.

You will probably have come up with the following reasons and perhaps many more:

- Not enough time.

- A lack of interest in the message.

- A negative reaction to the speaker.

- Mentally judging or arguing with points made by the speaker before he or she has finished talking.

- Being preoccupied with other matters.

- Becoming bored with listening and preferring active involvement by talking.

- The poor delivery of the message - monotone; lack of enthusiasm; poor articulation; no eye contact; etc.

A Conscious Effort

Listening requires a conscious effort. Imagine yourself at a social occasion standing around with a group of colleagues or friends, one of whom is telling a joke. Can you picture it? Now while you are standing there and the joke is being told, what is going through your mind? Most people when asked the same question say one of the following:

- *I was trying to work out the punch-line.*

- *I was trying to think if I had heard it before.*

- *I was thinking about how to get out of there.*

- *I was hoping I'd get it, and laugh with everyone else.*
- *I was mentally rehearsing my own joke.*

Okay, fair enough, this is only about listening to a joke but how guilty are you of not listening attentively in other circumstances? Our minds are continually active and to focus attention solely on what someone else is saying is not always that easy.

Notebook Exercise: What Could You Do?

What could you do that would make it easier for you to listen, and would also show the other person that you were listening? List your answers in your notebook before reading any further.

Compare your answers to these suggestions:

- Face the person who is talking and maintain a comfortable level of eye contact.

- Maintain a physical distance that feels appropriate for both of you.

- Give your undivided attention and refrain from doing anything else at that time.

- Get rid of any possible interruptions.

- Concentrate on what they are saying. See it from their point of view and try to grasp the *meaning* of what they are saying.

- Stop any mental rehearsing you might be doing. Don't think of your next question or how you might reply. Try to understand what is being said at that moment.

- Wait three seconds after the person has finished talking before you say anything.

- Suspend your judgement about what they are saying.

- Listen with the intention of understanding what they are saying.

"You cannot truly listen to anyone and do anything else at the same time."

M. Scott Peck

Eye Contact

How do you feel when the person you are talking to isn't looking at you?

Even just improving your eye contact will have a positive impact on your listening skills. But how comfortable are you with maintaining eye contact? One of the exercises in our interpersonal skills training workshop is for people, in pairs, to face one another and maintain eye contact without talking. The level of discomfort is amazing! We have to keep telling people to stop talking and we don't even attempt to quieten the nervous laughter. Connecting with people *without* maintaining eye contact is extremely difficult.

Have you noticed that young children don't seem to have any problems maintaining eye contact? Picture a one-year-old boy sitting in a supermarket trolley, where his mum can keep an eye on him while she does her shopping. He seems to be comfortable staring at anyone. Hopefully you are the kind of person that responds by smiling or acknowledging him in some appropriately friendly way.

Why are children so uninhibited? One of the reasons is that they haven't yet been conditioned by experience or by a parent's familiar, *"Stop staring, it is rude."*

Unfortunately a lot of the conditioning imposed upon us by well-meaning parents hasn't been effectively updated. We are usually just left alone to figure it out for ourselves. *"Remember when I told you not to speak to strangers? Well you are twenty-seven now and..."*

Levels of Listening

Listening occurs on many levels, some of them not very effective at all. *'Not Listening'* is one level and *'Pretending to Listen'* is another. How often have you pretended to listen to someone? We naturally sense if someone is not really engaged with what we are saying regardless of their head-nodding or the so-called affirmative sounds they are making.

Paul Simon wrote the song, *'The Boxer'* in 1968 and in it expresses another level, *'Selective Listening'*, *"Still a man hears what he wants to hear and disregards the rest."*

And then there is *'Attentive Listening'* which is taught in schools, colleges and business training courses all over the world. Attentive listening has been described as paying attention and focusing energy on the words that are being said. Most business people have attended some kind of training where the following 'active-listening' techniques have been taught to improve listening skills:

- Face the person and maintain eye contact.

- Maintain an open body-posture; keep the palms of your hands facing upwards; unfold your arms; and lean slightly forward.

- Make appropriate facial gestures.

- Make acknowledging noises such as *'yes'*, *'I see'*, *'okay'*, *'uh-huh'*, *'right'*, etc.

- Nod your head.

It might surprise you to learn that consciously applying these behaviours is often the *cause* of bad listening skills. These techniques are usually derived from observing good listeners who actually do display these behaviours. The problem is that whilst you are focusing on what your hands are doing, or remembering to nod and make appropriate noises when the other person is speaking, your attention is on yourself, not on what the other person is saying.

Intention

Intention is the key. It is a certain mental process that drives good listeners to behave the way they do and this leads us to the most effective level of listening, *'Listen to Understand'*.

When you listen to understand, your intention is simply to try and understand what the other person is saying.

Most people listen from their own perspective; in other words from a point of, *"How does this affect me?"* It would be far more effective to strive to understand the other person's point of view and listen from *their* perspective, not your own. How is what they are saying affecting *them?* How are *they* feeling about what they are saying?

Body Language

If your intention is focused on *their* perspective and you are trying to understand what they are saying, you will *really* be listening. If you are listening to understand, your body language will also be naturally appropriate. In other words, you will be facing the person, maintaining eye contact, making appropriate sounds, etc., and all of this will be perceived as genuine by the talker - because it is.

Stop Multi-Tasking!

You don't save time by multi-tasking when communicating with others. For example, it is common for people at work to combine speaking to people with other tasks, thinking that this will save them precious time.

When people approach your desk and you don't give them your complete attention, they tend to go on and on and repeat themselves because they are not sure if you have heard or understood them. If you moved away from your computer, moved any paperwork aside, looked at them, and gave them your complete attention, they would more than likely appreciate that you were making time for them in a busy period. They would therefore get to the point much more quickly.

And then there is the reciprocal action. When you approach their desk, they would usually feel obliged to give you their full attention. Besides, working on your computer or looking at paperwork when someone is talking to you is just plain rude.

"Courage is what it takes to stand up and speak; courage is also what it takes to sit down and listen."
Winston Churchill

"When people talk, listen completely.
Most people never listen."
Ernest Hemingway

Summary

There are those that listen
And there are those who wait to talk

All these skills are centred on the Three Key Principles:

Enhance, or at least maintain, the self-esteem of others.

Listen and respond with empathy.

Involve others.

Are you just waiting for a chance to speak? Are your discussions more like a competitive sparring back and forth? No wonder we don't often feel understood. We aren't being listened to.

True listeners are noticed and respected. When you are listening to fully understand what someone is saying, you are indicating, at that moment, that they are more important than anything or anyone else. This is a fine example of enhancing self-esteem (Key Principle One).

Body Language

Appropriate body language is essential for effective communication. Show the other person that you are listening by facing the person and maintaining eye contact, etc. The point emphasised throughout this book is that if you are listening to understand, your body language will be naturally appropriate. In other words, you will be doing it automatically.

"The most basic of all human needs is the need to understand and be understood. The best way to understand people is to listen to them."

Ralph Nichols

"I know that you believe you understand what you think I said, but I'm not sure you realise that what you heard is not what I meant."

Robert McCloskey

Application

A Riddle for You

There were five birds sitting on a wire.

Three of them decided to fly away.

How many birds were left on the wire?

The three only decided to fly away, they didn't get around to it (the answer is five). When all is said and done, much more is said than done! Reading this book won't create change. You need to implement the skills as soon as possible, preferably within forty-eight hours of first reading them, in order to experience the magic.

- Set a goal to **listen to understand** and rate yourself out of ten after each conversation. Just the act of trying to understand will improve your listening skills and therefore have a significant positive impact on the quality of your relationships.

- Practise maintaining eye contact whenever talking to or listening to others.

- Take time to notice how often you interrupt, and even finish people's sentences for them. And then stop it.

- Imagine that whoever you are interacting with has something tattooed on his or her forehead which is an indication of what he or she really wants - it reads: *'Make me feel important'.*

- For Managers: Sit each of your people down and give them a damn good listening to!

"Prior to the internet, the last technology that had any real effect on the way people sat down and talked together was the table."

Clay Shirky

The Power of Involvement

The Communication Styles

*"Without involvement, there is no commitment.
Mark it down, asterisk it, circle it, underline it.
No involvement, no commitment."*

Stephen R Covey

Two Styles of Communication

The power of involving people is the key to establishing, nurturing, and maintaining long-term relationships.

People want to be included and involved. It makes them feel important. Why else would parents lift their young children to enable them to post a letter or press a button? How does it make the child feel? How do you feel when someone asks your opinion rather than forces their own upon you?

There are some great entertainers that are masters at involving others. Robbie Williams, for example, will keep moving around the stage to make sure that he interacts with all of the audience. At times he sings just the first few words and then holds the microphone out, inviting the audience to complete the line. He often asks them to take part by getting them to do things like 'bounce'. He shows them how to do it, watches them do it, and then gives them positive feedback, *"This is amazing!"* He gets the audience to do their fair share of the dancing and singing by telling them, *"I'm coming to watch you."* Then he counts them in and cups his hand to his ear to hear what they are singing, whilst at the same time making sure he involves the entire audience; *"At the back." "At the side." "Now all you beautiful people down here at the front."* He skilfully manages to involve and engage 70,000 people at a time.

Push and Pull

An involving communication style is referred to as a Pull Style as opposed to a Push Style. Some of the characteristics of a Pull Style include:

- A two-way conversation - Collaboration.
- High involvement.
- High engagement.
- High commitment.
- Always giving the other person a genuine choice.
- Self-enforcing.
- Seeking information by using Open Questions.
- Engaging the thinking of others.
- Listening to understand.
- Testing understanding.
- Always an 'Adult / Adult' interaction.
- Always a 'Win-Win' interaction.
- Quicker in the long term.

The characteristics of using a Push Style include:

- A one-way conversation. The focus is only on one's own agenda.

- Telling people what to do, how to do it, and when to do it.

- Good for providing needed instruction or direction.

- Can work well in the short term.

- Easy to use when one has the authority.

- Low involvement.

- Low engagement.

- Can appear aggressive, forceful, pushy, etc.

- Quicker to use in the short term, but much slower to get results in the long term.

- Needs constant reinforcement.

- Often a high-risk strategy.

- Use of Closed Questions.

- Often a 'Win-Lose' interaction which becomes a 'Lose-Lose' in the longer term.

- Often an 'Adult / Child' type of interaction.

Appropriateness

There are times when a Push Style of communication is appropriate, for example when a situation requires immediate action. In a work situation, there are many times a manager will provide an instruction that needs to be carried out quickly. Wherever possible an effective manager or leader would involve individuals, ensuring commitment to the results. If the manager uses a Pull Style whenever possible, trust is gained and then when a Push Style needs to be used, it is understood and accepted.

Using language to tell, push, coerce, and persuade people to do what you want them to do is using language to control and exert power over others. It is easy to use a Push Style when you have authority (do we *really* have authority over people in the long term?). The problem is that, if it works, it is usually only effective in the short term; needs constant reinforcement; can often be perceived as arrogant, aggressive, and selfish; and lacks the involvement of the other person, which is vital in gaining commitment. It does, however, have its place in reinforcing standards, reminding people of agreed behaviour, emergency situations, etc.

Summary

The key to gaining commitment and buy-in
is to involve others

When you listen with the intention of understanding, you are truly involving the other person. Use a Pull Style of communication to involve and engage the minds of others.

"Alone we can do so little; together we can do so much."
Helen Keller

"The secret is to gang up on the problem
rather than each other."
Thomas Stallkamp

"Tell me and I forget.
Teach me and I remember.
Involve me and I learn."
Benjamin Franklin

Application

- Commitment is gained by using a Pull Style of communication. Make an effort to involve others especially in decision-making.

- Be aware of how often you ask the opinions of others and make an effort to focus on their agenda rather than just your own.

- Keep practising eye contact whenever talking to or listening to others.

- Listen with the intention of understanding.

Questioning

"Beware of unchallenged paradigms."

Russ Baleson

Notebook Exercise:
Open and Closed Questions

Take a few moments to write down a couple of examples of Closed Questions and a couple of examples of Open Questions before reading any further.

Challenging the Paradigm

A paradigm is a theory or belief system that guides the way we do things. It can be defined as a pattern, a habit, or a model. A paradigm can also be described as a set of assumptions, concepts, values, and practices that constitute a way of viewing reality. It is easy to buy into a paradigm when it makes sense and you have no other reference. It isn't always the wisest thing to do.

> *If you always do what you have always done,*
> *you will always get what you have always got.*

In order to engage, involve, and connect with people, you need to be asking Open Questions and listening to understand their answers. Millions of people all over the world have been taught that Open Questions start with the words *'Who', 'What', 'When', 'Where', 'Why' and 'How'*. Do they really?

Another paradigm that many have bought into is that a Closed Question is one that provokes a *'Yes'* or *'No'* answer and therefore, if someone can't reply with a *Yes* or a *No*, then the question is Open. This is false logic.

The type of question does not depend upon how it is answered but rather on how well the intention of the question has been communicated.

You cannot control another's response. Sometimes a Closed Question will elicit a detailed response and vice-versa.

By understanding the purpose of an Open Question, you can give yourself the best chance of communicating your intention clearly, being understood, and receiving the type of response you are seeking.

Origin

The *'Five Ws and an H'* are questions which *are* effective in information-gathering. They are often mentioned in journalism, research, investigations, etc., about how to get the complete story on a subject. For example:

- *Who is it about?*
- *What happened?*
- *When did it take place?*
- *Where did it take place?*
- *Why did it happen?*
- *How did it happen?*

This style of questioning usually uncovers the facts necessary for a report to be considered complete. But let's not confuse this with the concept of asking effective Open Questions.

Intention

What is the intention of an Open Question? It is to draw out a more detailed response; to encourage someone to open up (we should refer to them as Open-Up Questions). But, in the spirit of crystal-clear communication, let's speak plainly - **The purpose of an Open Question is to get the other person to talk lots**.

Take a look at the following:

- *Who did you meet last night?*

- *What is your name?*

- *When did you get here?*

- *Where do you live?*

- *Why do you need to see him?*

- *How was school?*

Do any of the above questions clearly communicate the real intention of an Open Question? In other words, **do any of them say, *without ambiguity*, 'Talk lots to me'?** If there is any ambiguity, then there is a chance that the intention won't be clearly understood.

I am sure that you are familiar with the question, *"How was school?"* How do children respond when asked this question? Usually with an "Okay" or a "Fine".

They certainly don't see it as an invitation to talk lots about their recent school activities. And what's more, this question is often asked when the child's attention is occupied in some activity or when the parent is multi-tasking, possibly packing away the groceries for example. And so overall, there is no way that the question can be perceived as a genuine request for lots of information.

Consider the alternative of a parent waiting until the child is not involved in an activity, facing the child, maintaining a comfortable eye contact and asking, *"Tell me more about some of the things you've been doing at school lately; I'd really like to know how things have been for you."* The chance of the child opening up is much better than if the parent just asks, *"How was school?"*

It is Not the Word or the Phrase

Trying to replace the *'who'*, *'what'*, *'when'*, 'where', 'why', and 'how' with alternative words or phrases is another mistake that many make. *Describe* to me in detail, *tell me*, *talk me through*, etc. are all phrases that appear to be an effective way of communicating the concept of *'Talk lots to me'*. But if you are relying on a word or phrase to do the work for you, then you may as well revert back to the old paradigm.

If your intention is to get the person to open up to you, just think of the most obvious way you could communicate this in your own natural style. *"Describe to me absolutely everything you did this weekend,"* doesn't sound like a genuinely interested and natural approach.

Why Use Open Questions?

Good Open Questions can stimulate conversation, create comfortable rapport, allow freedom of expression (while you listen of course), and avoid the harsh interrogation style that using many Closed Questions creates.

"If you want a wise answer, ask a reasonable question."

Johan Wolfgang Von Goethe

Summary

Does it say, without ambiguity, "Talk lots to me"?

One of the characteristics of a Pull Style is the effective use of questioning. In order to be able to listen to understand, you first need to get someone to 'open up' and talk freely. And that is the purpose of an Open Question - to get the other person to talk lots.

The traditional Open Question paradigm does not necessarily communicate one's intention effectively. Truly successful people continually challenge paradigms. Think of how you can say, *"Talk lots to me,"* in a way that leaves no doubt at all about your intention.

"Insanity: doing the same thing over and over again and expecting different results."

Albert Einstein

"Always the beautiful answer who asks a more beautiful question."

E. E. Cummings

"Who questions much, shall learn much, and retain much."

Francis Bacon

Application

- Check the examples of the Open Questions you provided in the last notebook exercise. Do any of them say, without ambiguity, *"Talk lots to me"*? If there is any ambiguity, there will be a chance that your intention will not be understood, so rephrase them and notice the difference.

- Try it out today! Phrase a question in such a way that it is absolutely obvious that you want someone to talk lots, and notice the difference in response.

- Listen to understand. Remember that as soon as someone begins to respond to your question, your role needs to change to that of the *Listener* if you really expect them to open up to you. You will find it a very effective and worthwhile paradigm shift.

- Open yourself to new learning by making a habit of challenging your paradigms. Have fun with it. Experiment with questioning your typical routine. Take a different route to work. Sleep on the side of the bed you don't usually sleep on. The next time you buy a magazine or newspaper, buy one that you wouldn't normally read. You might be pleasantly surprised or, at worst, you might just confirm that your current habit is one that works best for you.

Appropriate Silence

"Don't you hate that? Uncomfortable silence. Why do we feel it's necessary to talk about bull in order to feel comfortable? That's when you know you've found somebody really special. When you can just shut the hell up for a minute and comfortably share a silence."

Pulp Fiction

Notebook Exercise:
When should you shut up?

Before reading further, make a note of when you believe it would be beneficial to remain silent.

Take a look at what you have written and ask yourself if you *do* keep quiet in those circumstances. My guess is that you probably don't.

What is it that makes you so uncomfortable with silence? Many people feel the need to fill the void of silence with needless chatter. Silence can be disconcerting and can make people feel uncomfortable, but the appropriate use of silence can also have a major positive impact on your gravitas and interpersonal skills.

It would be best to remain silent in the following circumstances:

When someone is talking

When someone else is talking they are certainly not listening to you, so what is the point of interrupting? Wait until they are completely finished before claiming the spotlight. All the reasons we interrupt are about ourselves. Make it more about them and you will naturally interrupt less.

When you have asked a question

Keeping quiet after you have asked a question adds gravitas; shows that you expect an answer; shows that you are interested in their opinion; and avoids the clumsiness of multiple questions. For example: *"How many people do you have working for you? Are they all qualified? Do you put them through an induction programme?"* Which question are you expecting the person to answer? Ask only one question and wait for an answer.

Keeping quiet after asking a question also ensures that your Open Questions remain open. So many people ask excellent Open Questions and then close them down by not waiting for an answer. For example: *"So tell me more about some of the problems you have been experiencing with your new system. How long has it been installed?"*

Many people also feel a need to explain their question which can make it seem complicated and difficult to follow. For example: *"How have you been marketing your new services? I mean how do you get the concept across to your target market? Do you use television advertising at all?"* Once again, just ask the first question and wait for an answer.

To allow or encourage someone to think
Keep quiet to give people a chance to reflect on what you have just said. Give your message a chance to sink in.

To add impact or gravitas
Pause for a few seconds to allow significant points to sink in.

When you don't have anything worthwhile to say
Enough said.

Notebook Exercise:
The Three-Second Rule

The three-second rule is: Wait three seconds after the other person has finished talking before you begin to talk. If you did this, how would it help? Make a note in your notebook before reading any further.

Waiting three seconds before you begin to speak:

- Gives you time to think.

- Shows the speaker that you are listening.

- Prevents you from reacting emotionally and impulsively.

- Allows others to finish what they have to say.

- Encourages others to tell you more than they would have done.

- Adds gravitas to your message.

- Makes it easier for you to cope with difficult situations.

- Gives you time to try and understand what is being said.

Please don't count to three when waiting to speak! You should be listening to understand what has been said and considering what you are about to say. When you are waiting to speak, three seconds can feel like a long time, but the other person is probably not even aware that there has been a gap in the flow of the conversation.

Please remember that too intense a silence will be uncomfortable and that is the opposite of what you are trying to achieve.

Summary

Wait three seconds after the other person has finished talking before you begin to talk.

Slow down. Communication is not a race. Be patient and become more comfortable with silence. Focus on what is happening in the moment rather than thinking about what you want to say.

The more you rush to be understood, the more likely it is that you will be interrupting and consequently taking much longer to have the same conversation.

Enhance the quality of your relationships. Show respect and maintain the speaker's self-esteem. Everyone loves to talk to someone who listens to understand what they are saying.

"When you become aware of silence,
immediately there is that state of inner still alertness.
You are present.
You have stepped out of thousands of years
of collective human conditioning."

Eckhart Tolle

Application

- Practise the three-second rule today. You will be pleasantly surprised at how effective it is and also how quickly you can get used to it.

- Listen to understand. Once again, if your intention is to listen to understand, you will automatically be waiting the three seconds.

- Find ways to get more comfortable with silence.

- Become aware of how often you interrupt to correct others or tell them about your experience. Let it go. Occasionally let them have the glory and notice the positive impact you create.

"Sometimes one creates a dynamic impression by saying something and sometimes one creates as significant an impression by remaining silent."

Dalai Lama

"Better to remain silent and be thought a fool than to speak out and remove all doubt."

Abraham Lincoln

Gravitas

Calm; professional; respectful; dignified; assertive; impact!

Your intention heard and felt

What is Gravitas?

Substance; weightiness;
A serious or dignified demeanour

Gravitas is a learned or acquired capability - a calm, steady, measured approach that earns attention and respect from others. Do you know someone who has natural gravitas? Think of those people who command respect by the way they present themselves.

I remember some of my school-teachers. There were those emotional, almost panicky individuals who constantly battled to control the class. Then there were those who caned us for the slightest transgression and so we behaved, but only out of fear, and we didn't necessarily learn much. But then there were those individuals who addressed us as adults in a confident, calm and steady manner. They earned our respect and attention.

And what about the parent who has something serious to address? It is natural to respond emotionally after having repeated the same messages day after day. But when parents purposely and calmly address a child's specific behaviour, in other words when they communicate with gravitas, they have an immediate impact.

Practical tips to help you project gravitas

The following tips will go a long way to help you:

- Be perceived as confident.
- Make an impact.
- Get taken seriously.
- Ensure that your message is delivered and understood as intended.

Ensure that your emotions are under control

It is not always practical to wait until you are completely calm before addressing certain issues, but it is important that you behave calmly when doing so.

Speak at a calm and measured pace

Practise speaking with gravitas (yes, it takes practice). At first it can feel strange speaking so slowly and deliberately but it won't appear strange to others.

Talk softly

It is not necessary to raise your voice to be heard. Speaking loudly or shouting often provokes a Defend/Attack response. (See the chapter on Handling Conflict for details on Defend/Attack.)

Use silence and pauses

- Become comfortable with silence before speaking, after you have made a point, and when you have said enough.

- Make an impact even before you open your mouth by considering what you are about to say before you say it. Start the interaction with a few seconds of eye contact and then once you have made the connection, begin to speak calmly.

- Pause for a few seconds to allow significant points to sink in. Ensure you maintain eye contact whilst doing so.

- When you have made your point, stop talking.

- When someone else is speaking, give them your undivided attention and try to understand what they are saying. Listening to understand will create a reciprocal gravitas.

- When the other person has finished speaking, don't rush to answer. Wait a few seconds and consider what they have said before responding (the three-second rule).

- If someone interrupts you, let them. It is pointless trying to talk when someone else is talking, and they are certainly not listening at that time. Wait until they are completely finished before speaking.

Maintain a relaxed and confident posture

Leaning forward might be perceived as aggressive, and slouching could be perceived as submissive. Relax and maintain a confident posture.

Face the person you are addressing

It is important to face the person you are addressing. Be on the same level (avoid physically talking down to people), and maintain eye contact.

Speak consciously

Are you making sense? Is your voice crisp and clear? Are you engaging with what you are saying? Become conscious of what you are saying and how you are saying it.

Less is more

A line in Robert Browning's poem *'The Faultless Painter,'* begins with, *"Well, less is more"*. This is also very true in terms of communication and gravitas. In other words, that which is less complicated is more engaging and better understood.

Once, when facilitating a feedback session a few weeks after running a workshop entitled, *'Managing Senior Stakeholders'*, I was given an example of the impact of simplicity.

Many of the delegates had already achieved excellent results from applying the skills learned in the workshop. One in particular had impressed the Sales Director so much that she had nominated him for the company's prestigious annual achievement award. When I asked him what he had done differently to make such a good impression, he said, *"I had always served her lobster thermidor, and all she ever wanted was chicken and chips."*

Keep it simple and to the point. It is more about the quality than the quantity.

*"Those who know what they are talking about
can afford to use words that everyone can understand."*

Eliminate 'Irritators'

*"Well, you know, like, at the end of the day, you know,
it's not exactly rocket science, if you know what I mean."*

Irritators are unconscious words or phrases that have the potential to irritate others. These words or phrases don't add anything to the communication and very often create a barrier. Many people find themselves unconsciously using Irritators as fillers because they are not comfortable with silence. This often undermines their intended communication. For example, as soon as someone says, *"With the greatest respect ..."* you can be sure that an insult is about to follow.

Irritators are normal; everyone uses them. Most people won't notice when you use them. But when you consciously eliminate them from your language, you immediately improve the impact of your message, the clarity of your intention, and your gravitas.

Be aware of using the following, and any other unconscious words or phrases. Listen to others, ask for feedback and record yourself. When you eliminate them, you will experience an immediate, positive impact. Also, be aware that *any* unconscious word or phrase that is used repetitively, for example, the overuse of the words *'actually'* and *'basically'*, can divert attention from what you are trying to say.

- *With respect.*

- *Don't take this the wrong way but....*

- *I'm not being funny but....*

- *Obviously* (for example: *"Obviously you'd agree"*).

- *At the end of the day* (it gets dark?).

- *But* (as in, *"You dealt with this quickly, but..."*).

- *I understand how you feel.*

- *It goes without saying.*

- *It's not rocket science.*

- *Let me level with you.*

- *To be honest...*

- *To be perfectly frank...*

- *You know / You know what I mean.*

- *You must understand that...*

Plus any unnecessary jargon, swearing etc.

Eliminate Unnecessary 'Softeners'

Assertive communication is impossible without eliminating unnecessary, and often unconscious, Softeners from your speech.

Good communication is clear, concise and to the point. Softeners can reduce the impact of your entire message. Look out for any of these unnecessary words and phrases when you are speaking. For example: *"I'm sorry to bother you but, I think that it would possibly be a little bit better, if you could perhaps, you know, if it's not too much trouble, send it to me directly, if that's okay with you?"*

Leaving out the unnecessary Softeners would communicate your message clearly and assertively:

"Could you please send it to me now so that I can work on it right away?"

Typical Softeners include:

- *I think* (when you are sure).
- *Sort of.*
- *Kind of.*
- *Perhaps.*
- *Possibly.*

There are situations when it is important to soften your message in order to be sensitive. There are, however, many times when it is inappropriate and undermines your assertiveness and credibility. When you project yourself positively and with gravitas, people will respond accordingly.

> *"I was always looking outside myself*
> *for strength and confidence*
> *but it comes from within.*
> *It is there all the time."*
>
> Anna Freud

Summary

People with gravitas tend to be noticed, listened to and respected. Gravitas relates to assertiveness and charisma. It conveys confidence and authenticity. It enables us to influence and inspire others. It is useful for leading others; coaching; training; selling; presenting; and negotiating; as well as for developing all kinds of relationships.

One of the reasons that people use Irritators is because they are not comfortable with silence and so they tend to fill it with words and phrases that not only detract from their personal gravitas, but also have the potential to annoy or alienate others.

Use gravitas to project confidence by:

- Ensuring that your emotions are under control.
- Speaking at a calm and measured pace.
- Talking softly.
- Using silence and pauses.
- Maintaining a relaxed and confident posture.
- Facing the person you are addressing.
- Maintaining eye contact.
- Speaking consciously.
- Eliminating 'Irritators' and unnecessary 'Softeners'.

"Confidence is contagious. So is lack of confidence."

Michael O'Brien

Application

- Take note of the typical Irritators that people use. This is not a pleasant task, but it is an important way of becoming aware of how Irritators diminish impact. It will also help to make you more conscious of the unnecessary words and phrases that you yourself use, some of which have the potential to irritate others.

- Record yourself and then listen out for any Irritators or Softeners so that you can replace them with silence.

- Slow down. Become conscious of the words you are using to convey your intention.

- Listen to understand.

"I used to use irritators all the time but now I, you know, avoid them like the plague. I wouldn't touch them with a barge-pole, if you know what I mean."

Testing Understanding

*Testing to make sure that you understand
what has been said or implied*

Testing Understanding

Notebook Exercise: The Benefits

Before reading any further, make sure you understand the intention of this skill.

**Testing to make sure that *you* understand
what has been said or implied.**

Now make a note of all the ways that using this skill could have a positive effect on your communication style. Please note that this skill refers to testing *your* understanding, not testing the understanding of others.

There are many benefits of Testing Understanding if it is done correctly. It is not about reiterating the speaker's words. It could sound quite stupid if you just repeated the words the speaker had used. *"I'm looking for a way to improve the morale in the office." "Oh, so you are looking for a way to improve the morale in your office?"*

It is also not about just using preambles such as, *"If I can just check my understanding, what you are saying is..."* or *"If I understand you correctly..."* When testing your understanding naturally, you might find yourself labelling your behaviour with something like, *"So what you are saying is..."* But the focus should always be on the intention of testing your understanding, not on using a phrase to apply a technique.

It is also not about paraphrasing what has been said. It is simply about testing to make sure that *you* understand what has been said or implied. And, please note, **you cannot test your understanding unless you have been listening to understand**.

So, for example, if you were in conversation with a colleague and he said, *"I'm not going to be there tomorrow,"* and you were crystal-clear as to what he meant or implied, then there would be no need to test your understanding. If you were not clear as to what he meant, you could test your understanding by saying, *"You're not going to be at the meeting?"*

Or, if you think he might be *implying* something (testing to make sure that you understand what has been said or *implied)*, you might say something like, *"Are you saying that it will be a waste of time?"*

The Benefits of Testing Understanding

Now let's refer back to the previous Notebook Exercise where you were asked to list the benefits of using this interactive skill. Remember that Testing Understanding is not a stand-alone skill. It is an integral part of your listening skills. Some of the many benefits are:

It ensures clarity

This is the obvious benefit. *"Are you saying that it will be a waste of time?"*

"No, it is going to be really worthwhile, you should definitely go. I would love to be there, but I have a meeting with a client."

It shows that you are listening

Once again, *you cannot test your understanding if you haven't been listening to understand*. It shows that you are trying to understand what someone is meaning or implying, not just listening to the words he or she is using. This is listening on a much deeper level.

It creates rapport and trust

It shows, without doubt, that you are interested in the other person by wanting to understand what he or she is saying. This level of interest and attention builds engagement and connection, and strengthens relationships.

It provides thinking time

We think much faster than we talk. If you test your understanding rather than immediately respond to what someone is saying, it will give you time to consider the most appropriate way to respond and avoid an impulsive or emotional reaction.

It helps you to remember what has been said

We tend to remember what we say a lot more than what we think. This is because, in addition to listening, we are also using the senses of speaking and hearing ourselves speak. In this way, the act of Testing Understanding helps aid retention.

It saves time and conflict

I am sure you have often heard someone say something like, *"No, I didn't want a full report, I just wanted a brief overview."* Testing Understanding would have clarified expectations and saved a lot of time.

It is a characteristic of a Pull Style

Using this communication skill, you are involving the other person, focusing on his or her agenda, and are therefore much more likely to build a good rapport.

"The noblest pleasure is the joy of understanding."

Leonardo da Vinci

Summarising as a Skill

Summarising is another behaviour that is very useful in gaining clarity. It is a behaviour which restates, in a shorter form, what has been discussed or agreed. This can take place at any stage of a conversation.

The Difference
Both Summarising and Testing Understanding are valuable skills in ensuring clarity of communication. The difference between them is their intention.

Summarising is a *statement* which aids clarity and ensures that the focus is kept on the agenda or on the main points of the discussion. Testing Understanding is a genuine desire to understand what has been said or implied and is, therefore, *always a question* requiring an answer.

Summary
"So far we have three suggestions, and we still need one more before we can structure the proposal."

Testing Understanding
"So far we have three suggestions, and we still need one more before we can structure the proposal?"

Summary

"Everyone hears only what he understands."
Johann Wolfgang von Goethe

You need to listen to understand before you are able to test your understanding. If you are trying to prepare a question to test your understanding while someone is still speaking, you have missed the point. If you just listen to understand, you don't even have to think about it. Testing will occur naturally as part of your focused attention and curiosity.

Don't check your understanding if it is perfectly clear what someone has said or implied. But, when it is necessary, the benefits of doing so are numerous.

- It ensures clarity.
- It shows that you are listening.
- It helps you remember what has been said.
- It provides thinking time.
- It creates rapport and trust.
- It saves time and conflict.
- It is a characteristic of a Pull Style of communication and builds engagement and relationships.

The skill of Summarising is another behaviour that is very useful in gaining clarity. The main difference is that Summarising is a statement, whereas Testing Understanding is a question requiring an answer.

Application

The next time you listen to someone, make sure that your attention is on what you think they mean or imply. Note how you naturally test understanding, but make sure that you do so at the right time without interrupting the flow of the conversation.

Recap

At this stage it is important that you go back and **read the Summary Page in each of the previous chapters.** This will help you to refresh and review the skills already covered and become aware of how they all interlock and support one-another.

> *"Any fool can know.*
> *The point is to understand."*
>
> Albert Einstein

Why?

"Because I said so!"

Why, oh Why?

What is the word used by most children that often frustrates their parents? The word *'why'*, of course.

Why do children keep asking why? Here are the most popular answers:

- Their minds are expanding and they are curious about the world.
- They are starting to understand the concept of cause and effect and finding out that there is a reason for almost everything.
- They are seeking attention.
- They are trying to engage their parents in conversation and keep them talking for as long as possible.
- They want more information.

These are the logical and expected answers, but one of the main reasons that children keep asking why, *is because they are not told why!*

Few parents explain the reasons for their everyday requests. *"Pick up your toys." "Put that down." "Go and wash your hands."* How is a child supposed to know what a parent's reasons or intentions are? No wonder children are always trying to find out the reason for the request. This habit tends to tail off as the child gets older and is often as a result of a parent's continued and frustrated response, *"Because I said so, that's why!"*

If the request included a reason, there would be a much quicker satisfying of a child's curiosity and a deeper understanding of why things need to be done. For example:

"Pick up your toys from the carpet so that we can use that space to cover your school-books."

"Put that down please, I'm worried that it might break."

"Go and wash your hands, we are going to eat supper and your hands are still dirty from playing in the garden."

This is not a book on parenting, but the same concept holds true for adults. I was once asked to help a sales manager improve a disappointing attitude-survey rating. This was surprising, as he was viewed as competent by his own manager but, somehow, his staff did not hold the same opinion. After some discussion, we agreed that I would sit in on some of his one-to-one meetings with his team members as well as attend a team meeting, and then give him feedback of my observations.

Once we had agreed the date, I asked him what time the team meeting would begin. *"At ten,"* he answered.

"Why at ten?" I asked.

"Well some of the team have to travel from the South Coast and the journey can take them over an hour. I don't want them to have to get up at the crack of dawn just to get to a meeting. And if they do leave early they will hit the rush-hour traffic, which will take them even longer."

"And what have you told them about your reasons for starting at ten?" I asked.

"Nothing; I just told them that we start at ten."

It turned out that no one was aware of his considerate nature because he didn't explain his reasons. Once he changed his style and included a 'why' in his communication, they got to understand his intentions.

> *"No, no! The adventures first,*
> *explanations take such a dreadful time."*
> > Lewis Carroll

> *"The best argument is that*
> *which seems merely an explanation."*
> > Dale Carnegie

Summary

Our intentions and reasons seem so logical to us that we assume that they are perfectly clear to everyone else. This is often not the case.

To ensure clarity of intention, make sure you always provide a 'Why'. When we neglect to offer an explanation, our communication style can appear pushy. For example, note the difference between being told, *"Sit over there,"* and, *"Sit over there because the other chair is broken"*. We often assume, incorrectly, that our intention is common sense, or so clear that we don't need to provide an explanation.

Application

Make sure that you explain your reasons.

"Why?" I hear you ask!

So that your full intention is communicated and people will get to understand the kind of person you are much more quickly.

Feedback

*Behaviour that is rewarded
will be repeated*

Providing Feedback

Four-year-old Arthur had just spent three hours in his bedroom teaching himself how to tie his shoelaces. He finally came running out and said, *"Daddy, Daddy, look! I can tie my own shoelaces!"* And his father replied, *"Tuck your shirt in, Arthur."*

Managers, and people in general, have a natural inclination to look for the things that are wrong. Managers in particular are natural trouble-shooters and are always on the lookout for problems, difficulties, faults, dangers, etc. Most managers don't naturally look for what is right. And it seems that many also find it a bit embarrassing to provide positive personal feedback.

Providing effective positive feedback is the easiest and most motivating way to shape someone's behaviour.

If you are a manager and feel a bit hesitant about telling people what you like about them or what you like about what they are doing, then get over it! This is an essential part of your role, and once applied, will not only motivate others, but will make you feel good too. But this is not just a skill for managers. It is something that anyone can use to influence and shape the behaviour of others.

The Way of the Tongue

If we have a natural inclination to look for the things that are wrong, how do we keep ourselves and others positive, especially in challenging times? How do you build and maintain your confidence when life can seem so difficult? Well... it all depends upon how you look at it.

At the end of the nineteenth century, many shoe manufacturers sent their representatives to Africa to study the prospects for expanding business. Almost all returned with the same answer, *"Nobody in Africa wears shoes."* The Bata shoe representative, however, returned with this message, *"Wonderful business opportunity, they have no shoes!"* It all depends upon how you look at it.

What do you think of the following statement?
Opportunitiesarenowhere

What statement do you see?
Opportunitiesarenowhere

Is this what you see?
Opportunities are nowhere

Or is this what you see?
Opportunities are now here

It all depends upon how you look at it. But most people are naturally inclined to look at things in a certain way.

The Mind is Like the Tongue

The mind is very much like the tongue in the way that it processes information. What do you do with your tongue? (No answers on a postcard, please!)

You move your tongue around your mouth and examine your teeth without even realising that you are doing so. I doubt that you have ever made a conscious decision to carry out a routine tooth-check with your tongue. You are, however, very conscious of what you are doing when you discover a bit of food stuck in a tooth, or when you feel the sharpness of a rough edge. The tongue, like the mind, is continually looking for problems, and tends to find them.

Think about it; your tongue doesn't stop until it finds something wrong. It doesn't take any notice of what is good. You never stop during this dental examination to say, *"Mmmm, that's a nice tooth, it's so smooth."* No, like the mind, your tongue tends to look for and notice what is wrong, not what is right. Being aware of this gives us an opportunity to do something about it.

How do you Train Your Mind?

So, if the natural tendency of the mind is to look for problems, what can you do about it? How can you train your mind? It is quite simple, really. Get the tongue looking for and acknowledging the good teeth! Make yourself aware of all the wonderful, good, positive things in your life and express gratitude for them.

You can begin by giving *yourself* some feedback. Dedicate a few minutes every day to acknowledging what you have done well, what you are grateful for, and what you appreciate about your life. The next Notebook Exercise will show you how quick and simple this is to do, but don't skim over it! Putting it into action is the only way to experience the effect.

Notebook Exercise: Feedback to Myself

Make a note of three things you have already done well today and then say them out loud. Do it right now and see how it feels.

1.
2.
3.

When complete, make a note of at least three things you are grateful for and then say these out loud.

1.
2.
3.

How do you feel? If you can get yourself to focus on all the good things that you usually take for granted, you will build up a positive appreciation of healthy psychological functioning which will give you an inner-belief of strength and realistic balance. This is especially useful when times get tough. Invest a few minutes every day for a week acknowledging what you did well and what you are grateful for, and I *bet* you'll make it an ongoing practice.

In order to be able to give positive feedback to others, you will also have to train yourself to *look for* the positive in them and what they are doing.

Sincerity

We are good at sensing, even on an unconscious level, the underlying intentions of others. So don't even attempt to provide positive feedback if you are not being totally genuine about it. This type of cheap flattery and manipulation can easily destroy relationships.

There could even be a problem if you *are* being sincere. Imagine that a man reads this chapter and realises that he should be giving more positive feedback. The next day he notices and admires the hairstyle of one of the women in his office. He remembers how important it is to be genuine and, considering that he really does like her hairstyle, he walks up to her and says, *"Hi, your hair looks really good today."*

Ladies, imagine that you are at work and some man walks up to you and says, *"Hi, your hair looks really good today."* What is the first thing that you think? What does he want? Doesn't it usually look good?

If he had said *why* he believed her hair looked good, he would have had a much better chance of his compliment being perceived as intended. Let's take a look at a method for communicating positive feedback in a way that also communicates sincerity.

Positive Feedback

Most people understand the concept of *'Behaviour that is rewarded will be repeated'*. That is how we train animals, and we have a natural tendency to 'train' children in the same way. Think about what a parent does the first time a child uses a potty. Why does the parent clap excitedly, laying on the praise as if it is the best thing he or she has ever seen? Part of the reason is it that they are proud, but it is also because they are relieved that the nappy phase is almost over. They realise that this will make their lives a lot easier and that positive feedback will ensure that this specific behaviour is repeated.

It is very important that the feedback is behaviourally specific. Telling a child, for example, that he has been a good boy and expecting him to know the specific behaviour to repeat, is pointless. The same is true for adults. Praising a salesperson, for example, by saying, *"Well done, that was a brilliant sale,"* provides no substance whatsoever for the salesperson to judge the sincerity of the message, and certainly no indication of the behaviour required to repeat the success.

How to Provide Feedback Effectively

All relationships, as well as the coaching, training, leadership, and management of people, require the use of effective feedback skills. This feedback, to be constructive and effective, needs to be communicated in such a way that the person feels motivated to repeat successful behaviours, or improve an unsatisfactory performance.

What and Why

Positive feedback is specific information about what someone is doing well. To ensure your intention is communicated accurately, it is always important to provide a **'What'** and a **'Why'** in your feedback. In other words, the person must know exactly *what* was done well (the specific behaviour) and *why* you liked it. This will ensure that the feedback is seen to be sincere and that the specific behaviour is repeated.

For example:

"I really admired the way you kept calm with that customer. He was quite aggressive and yet you let him finish, acknowledged his disappointment and calmly offered to fix the situation for him. I am very impressed with the way you handle difficult situations with customers."

Be Direct and Personal

As with all the other communication skills, if you want someone to know your intention, you need to communicate it in a way that is obvious. Instead of implying positive feedback by saying something like, *"I like your shirt"*, make it much more personal by focusing on what you like about *the person* rather than his or her possessions. For example: *"You have such great taste in clothes, you always look good."*

And note the subtle difference between, *"Thanks for your advice, it really helped."* and, *"What I like about you is that you always take the time to listen. I really appreciate your help."* Please don't stop thanking people. A sincere thank-you is always appreciated, but a sincere and personal *what* and *why* is far more powerful.

Gravitas

To communicate your sincerity even further, take a moment to slow down, maintain eye contact, and deliver the feedback calmly and assertively. Your gravitas communicates the sincerity of your praise (if you are being sincere).

Feedback for Improvement

And what about the feedback that is not positive? Most people try to remove awkwardness and conflict from situations and therefore often avoid this type of communication in the fear that it might turn into confrontation. Some situations might feel awkward, but there is a way of communicating this kind of feedback that maintains the self-esteem of others (Key Principle One), and also has a good chance of enhancing the relationship.

Feedback for improvement needs to be specific information about **what** was done and **why** it was not effective. It must then be followed up with **what** the alternative could be and **why** it would have been better. For example: *"You told me about the dinner when I was rushing out to the car, so I had no time to check my diary. Instead, I'd prefer it if you would talk to me about arrangements when I was at home, so that I could check my availability."*

If you are providing feedback to someone reporting to you it is preferable, where appropriate, to pull the second *'what'* and *'why'* from the other person.

For example: *"I noticed that when the customer said they didn't understand, you repeated what you had just said and the customer was no clearer. What could you have done at that stage that would have helped you to get through to that customer?"* Once they have answered, ask, *"And how would that have helped?"* This gets them to provide the second *'what'* and *'why'*.

Maintaining Self-Esteem

Remember Key Principle One? Enhance, or at least maintain, self-esteem. By providing feedback for improvement in the format above, the *'what'* ensures that the focus is placed on a specific behaviour rather than on a person's character. Consider the difference between, *"What's wrong with you? You are so unreliable!"* and, *"You said you would bring me the report by five and you only left it on my desk at six, so I didn't have the stats I needed for the meeting."*

The Psychology of Feedback

Picture the following scene. Imagine that during a business meeting in the city, the office manager summarises the progress made and says, *"We have done really well over the last few days. We have completed everything we planned and will finish this meeting well ahead of schedule. I realise that many of you have children in play groups and after-school care, so why don't you go and collect them right now whilst the traffic is still manageable? Bring them back here and we will have a room ready for them. While they are playing in their room, we will go into the boardroom and have a celebratory drink and final chat. It will only take about half-an-hour and then you can all leave directly for home without the hassle of navigating the traffic across town."*

Let's say that there are about nine children in total, boys and girls, ages ranging from five to eleven. The parents go and collect their children and, realising that this is the first time that they will be taking them to their place of work, they 'have a chat' with them before they arrive back at the office.

What do you think they will say to their children? What do you think the typical parent would say to their children in these circumstances? These are some of the responses suggested by our training course delegates:

- *I want you to behave.*
- *Don't draw on the walls.*
- *Don't interrupt us.*
- *Don't make a noise.*
- *Be a good boy.*
- *If you're good, we will stop off at Ley's on the way home and get you your favourite ice-cream.*

Setting Expectations

Let us take a quick diversion to examine the effectiveness of this type of communication. When you ask someone to do something, you are attempting to communicate your expectations of them. How effective do you think these parents have been in setting expectations? What does, *"I want you to behave"* mean? Does the child even try to work out what the parent means?

And what about all those *don'ts?* It is quite strange how we often try and motivate someone on the reverse of an idea. Some of us are more visual than others, but we all think in pictures. Why is it that we typically paint a picture of what we *don't* want to happen, and expect someone to work out our expectations by imagining the complete opposite? You can imagine what the child is hearing and picturing when they hear, *"Don't Draw on the walls."*

Let's get back to the scene. The children are all playing in the room allocated to them and the adults are in the boardroom. What do you think is going to happen? Will the children interrupt their parents with the usual, *"Dad,* (in a sing-song voice of course), *when are we going home?"* Of course they will.

And how will the typical parent react to this and other such interruptions. I'm sure you can imagine. Anything from, *"What did I say would happen if you didn't behave?"* to *"It won't be long now; here is some money, go and get yourself something nice from the dispensing machine."*

But let us imagine for a minute that the adults have been sitting in the boardroom for ten minutes and there have been no interruptions and absolutely no noise coming from the room that the children are in. What would the typical parent do? Yes, they would go and check. And let us imagine that they go and check, and to their amazement, the children are being really well behaved. They are chatting quietly amongst themselves and seem to be quite happy doing so. Of course the suspicious parents check a few times, and then what do they do? Correct, they go back to the boardroom.

Behaviour that is rewarded gets repeated

Unfortunately, even undesired behaviour that is repeated gets rewarded! We typically get this the wrong way around. When the children are misbehaving they are 'rewarded' with the attention that they are probably seeking. When they are doing exactly what we want them to do, we ignore them. It would have been so easy for a parent to take a moment with his or her child to say something like, *"I am really proud of you. You gave me your word that you wouldn't interrupt us and you have kept your word.*

I also love the way that you are sharing your toys with the other children. It means a lot to me, thank you." Now the child knows exactly what behaviour is appreciated and expected in the future. It works exactly the same way with much taller children.

Sarcastic Praise

So many people, for some reason or other, communicate praise in a way that is usually perceived as criticism. I have often heard people reward desired behaviour with a rude and sarcastic comment. *"Oh, so you do know how to load the washing machine!"* And that is supposed to inspire the person to load the washing machine in the future? I think not.

There are always opportunities to provide feedback if you look for them. The feedback doesn't have to be long and detailed. Even a quick 'what' and 'why' in the form of, *"That's a good idea Reinette, that way we will save a lot of time,"* will shape behaviour and improve a relationship.

Life Changing

The impact of feedback can be life-changing. Take, for example, Stephen King, one of the best-selling authors of all time. When he was six years old he wrote a story about four magic animals and gave it to his mother to read. This is how he relates part of the story.

"'You didn't copy this one?' she asked when she had finished reading it. I said no, I hadn't. She said it was good enough to be in a book. Nothing anyone has said to me since has made me feel any happier."

Accepting Positive Feedback

Many people feel uncomfortable receiving positive feedback. They tend to brush it off by saying things like: *"It was nothing." "I was just doing my job." "Oh it wasn't such a big deal."* The way to accept positive feedback is simply to say, *"Thank you"*. The other person has made an effort to acknowledge you and the least you could do is to accept it graciously. When you say thank you, you are not saying, *"Thank you, yes I am great."* You are simply saying thank you for the feedback.

If you keep brushing it off, don't be surprised if you start receiving less and less positive feedback. If you make it difficult for people to say good things to you, they will soon stop.

Summary

There are several guidelines to bear in mind when giving effective feedback:

- Don't pay compliments just to make someone feel good. Your intention needs to be honest and sincere. Don't say that something was done well when it wasn't and, if you can't think of anything good to say, keep quiet.

- Feedback must be delivered with gravitas. Delivering compliments calmly, at a measured pace, and with eye contact, will communicate your sincerity and ensure your intention has the best chance of being correctly perceived.

- We often give feedback based on results; this doesn't have the same impact as behavioural feedback. Don't respond too quickly with feedback until you know exactly what the person has done (rather than just the results achieved). Ask questions and listen carefully to *how* they have achieved it, and then you can reinforce the specific behaviour.

- Don't ever use the words, *'but'* or *'however'* when giving feedback. It is annoying, disrespectful and manipulative. Trying to hide uncomfortable feedback within positive feedback makes the good feedback appear insincere. So many managers have been taught the *'Pat-Kick-Pat'* approach to providing feedback, or perhaps you know it as the *'Sandwich Technique'* (and if you know what most people call it, you will realise that I am being polite).

This is the technique of starting with positive feedback; sneaking in the negative feedback, and then quickly ending with more positive feedback. Even though this is a management technique that is taught all over the world, it always annoys and irritates people and therefore achieves the opposite effect to that intended.

Keep the two types of feedback separate. If your intention is to give positive feedback, give it anywhere and in front of anyone. If you want to give feedback for improvement, give it privately, in a calm manner, focusing on the specific behaviour rather than on the person's character.

- Don't give vague or unsupported feedback. Always supply the reason. Be specific about *what* was said or done and *why* you feel the behaviour was effective.

- When offering Feedback for Improvement, tell, or ask the person *what* could have been said or done that would have been better and *why* it would have been better.

  - *What* was done and *why* it wasn't effective.
  - *What* could have been done and *why* that would have been better.

- Always maintain the person's self-esteem.

- Don't focus only on very good or very bad behaviour. Examine the average performance as well and provide feedback for any effort or improvement. Providing behavioural feedback when someone is making an effort will help them achieve the goal much faster than without it.

"Too often we underestimate the power of a touch,
a smile, a kind word, a listening ear,
an honest compliment,
or the smallest act of caring,
all of which have the potential
to turn a life around."

Leo Buscaglia

"Feedback is the breakfast of champions."

Ken Blanchard

Application

- Try this at home! These interpersonal skills are effective with anyone in any situation and will have a significant positive impact on all your relationships.

- Make a list of those people, who, at any stage of your life, gave you some form of positive feedback that had a significant impact.

- Make a list of those people who deserve feedback from you and next to each name, list the date when you will be giving them the feedback (in a *what* and *why* format, of course).

- Read the following quote by author Stephen Levine and diarise a few more actions that this might prompt you to take:

> *"If you had an hour to live*
> *And could only make one phone call,*
>
> *Who would you call?*
>
> *What would you say?*
>
> *And why are you waiting?"*

Empathy

"Before you criticize a man, walk a mile in his shoes.
That way, when you do criticize him,
You will be a mile away,
and have his shoes."

Steve Martin

Empathy

Empathy - from Greek empatheia
(from em- *in* + pathos *feeling*)

People often confuse the words *Empathy* and *Sympathy*. Empathy is the experience of understanding another person's condition from their perspective, whereas sympathy refers to feelings of pity and sorrow for someone else's misfortune.

When you sympathise with someone, you are agreeing with their feelings, whereas when you empathise, you are not necessarily agreeing with them, you are just trying to understand them.

From *Their* Perspective

When people listen, they do so naturally from their own perspective. The concept of listening and responding with empathy (Key Principle Two) begins with the intention of understanding the other person's point of view from *their* perspective, not one's own. How is what they are saying affecting *them*? How do you imagine *they* are feeling about what they are saying? Communication is driven by intention, not technique, so be clear on your *intention* when you are listening and responding with empathy.

Don't Put Yourself in Their Shoes!

"I understand how you feel." "Oh no you don't!"

How do you feel when somebody tells you that they understand how you feel? Most of the time it's annoying, even though the person might be genuinely empathic. Take, for instance, a man using that approach to empathise with a pregnant woman. I think that flight would be the best immediate strategy.

We have learned to communicate empathy in some strange ways. We have been taught to imagine how we would feel if we were in a similar position to someone else and that would help us to empathise with them. If you were to empathise by asking yourself, *"How would I feel if I was that person?"* you have missed the point. It really isn't about you at all.

What is it about the word Eimpathy? Did you notice the incorrect spelling? There is no 'I' in Empathy and *that is the key*. When you put yourself in someone else's shoes, you are typically trying to imagine how you would feel if you were in that person's place. But there is no 'I' in Empathy. In other words, it is not about you, it is about them. So, once again, here is another paradigm to challenge. This concept of putting yourself in someone else's shoes misses the point of empathising.

Listen First

You can't respond with empathy
Unless you have been *listening with empathy*

You first need to listen and try to understand how someone is feeling before you can respond appropriately. Instead of saying, *"I understand how you feel, it happened to me too,"* simply consider how you think he or she is feeling and check it out. For example: *"You seem to be quite worried about how long it is taking?"*

When responding with empathy, you need to relate back both the **feeling** and the content **(about what)**. For example: *"You must be feeling very frustrated* (feeling) *that you weren't considered for the position?"* (about what).

In our quest to help others, we often rush to give advice or suggest a course of action when, most of the time, providing empathy would be far more appropriate. Some people compound matters even further by using the irritating phrase, *"If I were you, I would..."* Always check if someone wants advice before giving it to them.

Here are some more examples of responding with empathy:

- You seem to be *concerned* about how it will impact on your customers?
- You seem quite *excited* about meeting your nephew?

- It must be *frustrating* not having enough time to complete the project?
- You must be *annoyed* that he didn't consult you first?
- You seem *disappointed* that they didn't use your design?
- You seem quite *sad* that he's gone?
- You seem *delighted* that you no longer have to work in that office?
- You seem *relieved* that he finally saw your point of view?

Workshop Exercise

Here is one of the exercises we use in our Interpersonal Skills workshops which lets people experience the impact of Key Principle Two - listening and responding with empathy.

We begin the exercise by asking a volunteer to sit at the front of the group and relate a personal story about something significant that has happened to them. The volunteer must talk for a few minutes and try not to express any feelings or emotions that he or she had experienced at the time - not an easy thing to do for an expressive person. The rest of the delegates are asked to listen to understand what the person is saying and, at the same time, try to imagine how the person is feeling about what he or she is saying.

Then they are told that, as soon as the person has finished talking, they will be asked to pick up a pen and quickly write down the most significant *feeling* they imagined the person was experiencing, and *about what* they thought that feeling related to. For example, *'relieved that he was safe'* or *'worried that she would fall'*.

During the exercise, the facilitator interrupts the conversation briefly to point out the natural body language of the delegates. They are made aware of how their complete attention is on the person speaking. They are all facing the speaker and maintaining eye contact and there is no fidgeting. In other words, they have experienced the level of mental concentration that it takes to listen with the intention of understanding. They are also now aware of how their mental focus, their intention, ensures that their body language is naturally appropriate.

Once the person has finished talking, the delegates are allowed ten seconds to note down quickly the *feeling* and *content* as previously instructed.

This is stage one of the exercise. They have all practised and experienced the concept of *'listening to understand'*. The next stage is for them to check out their assumptions. In other words, to respond with empathy. So, one by one, they address the speaker and test their understanding of how they think he or she must be feeling.

"You must have been devastated when all of your hard work amounted to nothing?"

"You seem to have been worried that the rescue team wouldn't be able to find you?" Etc.

And then the connection begins! The response from the speaker is always enthusiastic, with a desire to elaborate even further on the incident. The positive effect of listening and responding with empathy is immediate.

Summary

The second Key Principle is: Listen and respond with empathy.

Listening with empathy and responding appropriately are two of the most powerful techniques you can use to develop your communication skills and improve your relationships. Being understood is a fundamental psychological need that we all have. A well-communicated empathic response will clearly show the other person that you are sincere, completely attentive, and trying to understand what they are saying and feeling.

Take time to listen to understand, and experience an immediate positive impact.

"Self-absorption in all its forms kills empathy, let alone compassion. When we focus on ourselves, our world contracts as our problems and preoccupations loom large. But when we focus on others, our world expands. Our own problems drift to the periphery of the mind and so seem smaller, and we increase our capacity for connection - or compassionate action."

Daniel Goleman

Application

There are many natural opportunities to respond with empathy; for example, to avoid a common mismatch in communication between couples. When a woman is talking about what happened to her that day, the well-intentioned male usually responds by offering advice. *"What you should do is..."* Most of the time, listening and responding with empathy would be more appropriate and a much-appreciated response.

In order for you to practise the art of responding with empathy, you first need to listen with empathy, or listen to understand. The next time you listen to someone, make sure that your attention is on what you think they are feeling about what they are saying, and then you will be in a position to empathise if it is appropriate to do so.

Feelings Commentary

*"Vulnerability
is the birthplace of innovation,
creativity and change."*

Brené Brown

Engagement / Connection

My first trip back to South Africa, after living abroad for seven years, taught me a valuable lesson about the spirit of community and connection.

I had just arrived in Johannesburg and needed a SIM card for my phone. Walking into a supermarket, I noticed the SIM cards displayed on a board next to the cashier - a large, elderly Zulu woman. I walked up to her, pointed to the SIM cards and asked her if I could take a look at one of them. She looked right at me, not at the SIM cards as I had expected, and said, *"And how are you?"*

I had definitely been away too long. Quite embarrassed, I replied, *"I'm sorry mama, I have forgotten my manners."* She smiled at that and so I asked, *"Should I try again?"*

"It is best," she replied.

I took a few steps back and once again walked towards her, and this time asked, *"Hi, how are you?"*

"Me, I'm fine. My legs are a bit swollen but I am working, and my children have got food. How are you?"

"I'm fine thanks. I have just arrived from the UK and I'm quite excited to be back in Jo'burg."

"Well welcome back; now, how can I help you?"

Consider the habitual exchange that usually takes place upon greeting; for example: *"Hi, how are you? Did you have a good weekend?"* I find that when I get to towns and villages far away from major city centres, some people actually want to know how I am and wait to hear my answer. But in general it seems that greetings are typically more of an unconscious ritual, and fail to create any meaningful connection.

"Good Morning!" said Bilbo, and he meant it.
The sun was shining, and the grass was very green.
But Gandalf looked at him from under long bushy eyebrows
that stuck out further than the brim of his shady hat.
"What do you mean?" he said.
"Do you wish me a good morning,
or mean that it is a good morning whether I want it or not;
or that you feel good this morning;
or that it is a morning to be good on?"

J. R. R. Tolkien

Once we get past the initial greeting, engagement doesn't necessarily follow. For example, one-to-one and group business meetings can be quite impersonal and tend to focus mostly on facts and information. It is only when we focus more on the person - on opinions, attitudes and emotions - that a deeper level of engagement can take place. There is always an element of risk involved when sharing feelings but the pay-off is the creation of deeper trust and rapport.

Enquiring about opinions or feelings, and listening and responding with empathy, is a way of showing a personal interest in someone and much more likely to engage their attention. Another way is to let them know how you are feeling - a Feelings Commentary.

Feelings Commentary

One of the most destructive elements in a relationship is our inability to relate what we are feeling. A *Feelings Commentary* is an extremely effective way of building trust, strengthening relationships, and communicating openly and assertively.

It is also known as 'responsibility language'. Instead of saying something like, *"You make me angry,"* it is better to take ownership of the communication by talking about how you are feeling and about what it is that is making you feel that way. For example: *"I'm feeling quite angry that you forgot to bring the tickets after I reminded you to do so."*

Because it is an honest communication of how you are feeling, and not just a criticism or attack, it shows your openness and willingness to talk constructively about an issue, which usually encourages openness and trust from the other person.

The 'Keys'

The two key elements in a Feelings Commentary are the same as in a statement of Empathy.

'Feeling' and *'About What'*

When responding with empathy, the focus is always on the other person's feelings; for example: *"You seem to be worried about how long it will take?"* When expressing a Feelings Commentary, it is always about how *you* are feeling. For example: *"I'm feeling quite uncomfortable about what happened at our last meeting and I would like to find a way to avoid that happening again."*

Getting Through to Children

Have you noticed the response of most children when a parent is barking out typical commands, such as, *"Put that down!" "Bring me your homework."?*

I remember watching the movie *A Boy Named Charlie Brown* many years ago. I was initially fascinated, and then got frustrated every time a grown-up was speaking. Instead of normal speech, all you could hear was a horn-like sound, something like, *"Wah wah wah wah wah wah wah."* My take on this was that parents can say things at times that don't engage their children and often don't make any sense at all. And so the children 'tune them out'.

Think about it. What is a child supposed to answer when a parent asks, *"How many times must I tell you?"* And what about, *"Do you want a smack?"* (Perhaps: *"Yes, I think a smack would go down very nicely at this point."*)

Parents also tend to use language that could be part of a comedy script. For example:

- *"Just look at that dirt on the back of your neck!"*
- *"If you cut your toes off with that thing, don't you come running to me!"*
- *"Keep crying and I'll give you something to cry about."*
- *"Shut your mouth and eat your supper."*

We often speak impulsively without considering if what we are saying is going to help us achieve what we intend.

Children, however, do notice when a parent communicates calmly with gravitas. Consider for example, the following Feelings Commentary instead of an emotional outburst:

"I'm feeling a bit frustrated that you haven't brought me your homework to check, because I've asked you twice already. Please bring it to me now so that we can do it before you go to bed."

Or, *"I'm disappointed that you didn't do what you promised you would do. I thought we had a better relationship than that."*

Adult-To-Adult

And, of course, the same is true in adult communication. A Feelings Commentary is an excellent way of communicating sensitive issues; addressing uncomfortable situations; communicating upwards to senior management; and also communicating positive emotions. For example:

"I'm feeling motivated by the way we are working together lately; we are producing some really good work."

"I am quite excited about the new project; it is a great opportunity to be more creative."

"I'm a bit disappointed that you didn't approach me before you spoke to him. That is what we had agreed."

"I'm feeling a bit awkward because I'm not sure how to say this to you in a way that will sound supportive."

"I'm feeling a bit uncomfortable with this process. It seems as if we really have no option, so I don't understand why you're asking us."

Reveal to others that you are human and they will find it easier to be open and honest with you. Develop a deep trust by risking telling the truth about what you are feeling and thinking.

"Vulnerability is the birthplace of love, belonging, joy, courage, empathy, and creativity. It is the source of hope, empathy, accountability, and authenticity. If we want greater clarity in our purpose or deeper and more meaningful spiritual lives, vulnerability is the path."

Brené Brown

"The most human thing we have to do is to learn to speak our honest convictions and feelings and live with the consequences. This is the first requirement of love and it makes us vulnerable to other people who may not accept us as we really are. But this truth, our vulnerability, is the only real thing we can give to other people."

Father William DuBay

"Vulnerability sounds like truth and feels like courage. Truth and courage aren't always comfortable, But they're never weakness."

Brené Brown

"My vulnerability is my strength."

Russ Baleson

Summary and Application

- The next time you greet someone and ask how they are, do so consciously and wait to hear what they have to say.

- The next time you are feeling emotional about something and you want to communicate it effectively, consider using a Feelings Commentary.

- The two 'keys' to remember when using a Feelings Commentary are *Feeling* and *About What*.

Enhance, or at least maintain, the self-esteem of others.

Listen and respond with empathy.

Involve others.

Handling Conflict

Avoiding Defend/Attack

Defend/Attack

*Is it more important for you to be right,
or to be happy?*

When discussions become emotionally heated and value-loaded behaviours are used to attack or make an emotional defence, it is called a Defend/Attack. The result, whether one is defending or attacking, is always the same - it is negative and destructive.

Ego

The ego is that part of us that wants to be seen, heard and valued, and so we have a deep desire to be listened to and understood. This natural and mostly unconscious intention often drives us to clash with others as we strive to get our point across. Being understood and gaining positive attention is vital to our psychological well-being, but it is all eroded when we engage in Defend/Attack behaviour.

When someone is 'pushing your button' it is natural to want to push back, but, when you do, it is often at the expense of the relationship. It is important to understand what causes this conflict and how you can prevent yourself from getting hooked in this type of emotional exchange.

"Try and understand *my* point of view!"

Think back to the last time you were in some kind of disagreement or argument (a Defend/Attack spiral). Regardless of the words you were using, what you were really saying was, *"Listen to me and just understand my point of view, the way I'm feeling, and then you will understand that my point is valid and we can carry on as normal."* And what was the other person saying at the same time? *"Listen to me and just understand my point of view, the way I'm feeling, and then you will understand that my point is valid and we can carry on as normal."* Both are struggling to be understood but neither is listening to understand.

Listening is the key principle to help avoid conflict and Defend/Attack situations. Both parties are eager to be heard, seen and valued and so *it is important that you begin by striving to be the first to understand and only then, to be understood.* It doesn't work the other way around.

This is not easy when emotions are high and you want to make yourself understood. Most people listen from their own perspective; in other words from a point of, *"How does this affect me?"* To avoid a Defend/Attack, you first need to understand the other person's point of view and listen from their perspective not yours.

Is it more important for you to be right, or to be happy?

What is your intention in this kind of interaction? Are you attempting to find a solution or are you trying to lay blame or prove who is right or wrong? This energy of blame always makes a bad situation worse. Wanting to be right, or defending your position, takes a lot of energy and often causes conflict.

Defending oneself or attacking someone else is actually missing the point. It focuses on the person rather than on the issue. A Defend/Attack is always personal and, typically, provokes a retaliating attack or defence in response. For example:

"You never listen to what I am saying."

or,

"Hey! I was just trying to help."

A Defend/Attack is a 'Push Style' responding to a 'Push Style', and the result is that neither party wins. For example:

"You were the one who said he would be there!"

"Yes, but you were the one who forgot to tell me the meeting was in your office!"

A Defend/Attack is always destructive in some way, and usually spirals and causes major friction in relationships.

Imagine the following scenario - a husband arrives home and says...

Hi honey, I'm home (or words to that effect).	Simple statement.
Hi sweetheart, did you get the milk?	Simple question.
Did I get the milk? Give me a break. I've been on the road for two hours after working non-stop for ten hours and all you want to know is...	Defend/Attack (Try and understand how I am feeling!).
(Interrupting....) Hey! I just asked if you brought the milk.	Defending - the same impact as attacking - another way of saying, *"Don't give me a hard time."*
Just asked! You're nagging again.	Defend/Attack.
Nagging? As if you never nag. You're always nagging me about your shirts.	Defend/Attack.
Well why don't you just iron them instead of waiting for me to remind you?	Defend/Attack.

What! I can't believe you said that. Do you think I've got nothing to do but be your slave? What do you ever do for me?	Defend/Attack.
Oh, so who helped your mum with her garden on Saturday?	Defend/Attack.
About bloody time too! The first time in eleven years.	Defend/Attack.
Yes but I did it didn't I? You just can't ever give me credit when I do a good job, you're always......	And on and on and on......

Characteristics of a Defend/Attack

There are numerous Defend/Attacks in a typical heated discussion or argument - a spiral. But even just a single Defend/Attack can be destructive. Here are the main characteristics of this type of interaction:

It is always personal
A Defend/Attack is always personal. The intention is to blame, ridicule, deflate, or belittle the other person, even if done defensively. It is not a behaviour that will build, maintain, or nurture a relationship.

It is off the issue

And, after all that heated discussion, where's the milk? Did you notice that neither of the people in the previous interaction focused on the issue at hand (the milk)? So where did all the frustration come from? More than likely because they had not expressed issues appropriately at the time they occurred. The quicker an issue or behaviour is addressed, the easier it is to have the conversation.

It is always destructive

Who wins this type of argument? You might think you do; for example: *"No-one talks to me like that!"* (Yes they do, but you don't know how to handle it). Or, *"Ha, I really told her!"* (Yes, but now she's leaving you!).

Regardless of the situation, a Defend/Attack is *always* destructive and often spirals out of control. Even in humour, or what we often refer to as banter or 'Taking the Mickey', a Defend/Attack can hurt on some level.

I was once discussing the Defend/Attack concept with a group of delegates in an Interpersonal Skills Workshop and made the statement, *"Even in humour, a Defend/Attack can hurt on some level."* All of a sudden one of the delegates burst into tears. When I asked her if she was okay, she looked at her colleagues and, still sobbing, said, *"I am sick and tired of you always making fun of the way I ..."*

I didn't quite understand the rest of what she was saying, as it was difficult to make out her words in-between her sobbing. All of her colleagues appeared shocked and one of them looked at her and said, *"But we have been doing that for years, and you have always laughed."* And she replied, *"Will you all just stop it already!"*

Push - Push

A Defend/Attack is a Push Style responding to a Push Style, which is one of the causes of conflict. *"Yes but,"* is a typical example of this type of response. You can't get hooked into a Defend/Attack spiral if you are using a 'Pull' style. Most of the alternatives that follow are based on the Pull Style.

Alternatives to a Defend/Attack

Let it go!

If it is not important, let it go! And sometimes even when it is important, apologising doesn't mean that you were wrong or the other person was right. It just means that you value the relationship more than your ego. Most people argue, confront, and fight over practically anything, turning their lives into a series of battles over relatively insignificant issues. It makes more sense to choose your confrontations wisely and sometimes let others have the satisfaction of being right.

Listen to understand
You can stop the spiral of conflict and stubbornness by being the first person to reach out and listen. It is not a competition. Push your emotions aside and listen from their perspective, not yours. Consider how they are feeling and how what they are saying is affecting them.

Test your understanding
Ask questions to make sure you understand what the other person is saying, before even attempting a response.

Respond with empathy
They want to be understood as much as you do, and they aren't ready to understand your point of view until they feel understood. Responding with empathy shows that you are trying to understand. You can't respond with empathy unless you have been *listening* with empathy. In other words, you need to first listen and try to understand how they are feeling before you can respond appropriately. Simply consider how you think they are feeling and check it out. For example: *"You seem to be quite worried about how long it is taking?"* When responding with empathy, remember to relate back both the *'feeling'* and *'about what'*. For example: *"You seem to be annoyed* (feeling) *that I didn't get there on time?* (about what)*"* But don't be sarcastic! That would be just another form of Defend/Attack.

Wait three seconds

We often react to criticism emotionally and impulsively by saying the first thing that comes to mind. Waiting a few seconds after the person finishes talking will give you time to consider your reaction. It will also:

- Allow them to finish speaking.
- Give you time to try and understand what is being said.
- Give you time to consider what you really want from the transaction.
- Prevent you from reacting impulsively and emotionally.
- Help you to cope with difficult situations, especially when you need time to think of an appropriate and constructive response.

Appropriate Silence

Remember that too intense a silence will be uncomfortable and achieve the opposite effect.

Focus on the issue, not the person

Keep your focus on the topic at hand. Ask questions about the issue and seek or propose a solution.

Use a Feelings Commentary

For example: *"I'm feeling a bit concerned that this seems like an argument. I certainly don't want to argue with you; how can I help fix this?"*

"Is this the right room for an argument?"

"I told you once."

"No you haven't."

"Yes I have."

"When?"

"Just now."

"No you didn't."

"Yes I did."

"You didn't."

"I did!"

"You didn't!"

"I'm telling you I did!"

"You did not!!"

"Oh, I'm sorry, just one moment. Is this a five minute argument or the full half hour?"

Monty Python's Flying Circus

Summary

Nurture Relationships
Everyone has an inherent need to be heard, seen, and valued. Avoid getting hooked into *any* Defend/Attack situation. Enhance, or at least maintain, the self-esteem of others at all times and you can be assured of much improved relationships.

Characteristics of a Defend/Attack
- It focuses on the person rather than on the issue.
- It is personal.
- It is emotional.
- It is a Push Style responding to another Push Style.
- It is always destructive.
- It usually spirals and causes major friction.
- It will always result in a 'Lose-Lose' situation.

Alternatives to Defend/Attack
- Listen to understand (listen with empathy).
- Respond with empathy.
- Use a Pull Style of communication.
- Test your understanding.
- Ask questions.
- Stay focused on the real issue at hand.
- Use a Feelings Commentary.
- Apply the three-second rule - use appropriate silence.
- Let them finish talking.
- Apologise if you have been wrong.
- Let it go if it is not important.

Application

Be on the lookout for any potential disagreements, arguments, or complaints. Be aware of the moment you feel the need to prove yourself right and remind yourself that no-one wins a Defend/Attack. Use one of the many alternatives to find a solution and maintain the relationship.

"Don't raise your voice, improve your argument."

Desmond Tutu

"I am very cautious of people who are absolutely right, especially when they are vehemently so."

Michael Palin

Handling Complaints

Handling Complaints

People complain. We receive complaints from customers, colleagues, bosses, friends, partners, children, etc. The way we handle the situation has an immediate impact on the relationship.

Emotion

Many people get quite emotional when they complain, and some just *act* as if they are frustrated or angry. They seem to feel that unless they show and express their dissatisfaction, they won't be taken seriously enough to get the action needed to rectify the situation.

How do you deal with an angry or annoyed customer? The first step is probably the most difficult, because it requires patience. Imagine the following scene: A man walks into a shop holding up a pair of jeans and begins to shout, *"You sold this pair of jeans to my daughter! What right have you to ...?"*

He is so cross that he doesn't even realise that he has walked into the 'Pizza Crust' instead of the 'Jeans Store'! If you were working in the Pizza Crust, what do you think would happen if you tried to save him embarrassment by interrupting and telling him that he was in the wrong store? Correct; he would get even more angry.

Even someone who is absolutely wrong, if interrupted, will not be listening to you and will probably just get angrier. It is important that, no matter what someone is complaining about or how justified or not you think they might be, you let them finish completely before you intervene. If you do interrupt, you will be entering into a Defend/Attack situation, and let me remind you again - it is a no-win situation.

The Steps

The combination of the communication skills already covered, plus the following steps, provide an effective strategy to handle such situations.

1. **Listen to understand.**
2. **Empathise.**
3. **Apologise (without accepting or placing the blame).**
4. **Take action to rectify the situation (starting with a Pull Style of communication).**

1. Listen to understand

Listen to understand means applying all the skills already discussed in this book to ensure complete understanding of what is being said. It also means that you need to wait until the person is completely finished talking before saying anything.

2. Empathise

One of the reasons that the person is complaining is that they want you to understand how they are feeling about a certain situation. Responding with empathy shows that you are listening and that you are trying to understand how they are feeling. Remember that you must first listen to understand and then respond by feeding back what you think the person is *feeling* and *about what*. Listening to understand might take quite a while, depending upon the circumstances, but responding with empathy takes just a few seconds.

3. Apologise

Apologise means apologising (taking responsibility) for the situation without placing blame, accepting blame or making excuses. For example: *"I'm sorry this has happened."* It is more of an acknowledgement than an apology. If, however, you have made a mistake, own up to it, accept the blame, and apologise. This also takes a couple of seconds at most.

4. Take action to rectify the situation

This is where so many people make a mistake. They try and fix the problem by telling the customer what they are going to do. Imagine that the man described above was actually moaning about a pizza being cold and so, therefore, he was in the right place. And imagine the person in Pizza Crust responds to his complaint by saying, *"That must have been annoying, getting it home and finding it was cold. I'm sorry about that. What I will do for you is make you a pizza now, obviously at no charge, and I will also let you have one of our special delivery boxes free of charge, so that it will still be hot when you get it home."* And the customer responds, *"I don't want a pizza now!"*

So many companies offer some form of compensation without even knowing what the customer is wanting. You need to do something that the person *wants* you to do. In other words, use a Pull Style to find out what course of action the person requires.

For Example

After listening attentively, the conversation might go something like this:

"That must have been very frustrating - not getting it in time. I'm sorry about that. How can I help?"

This technique can be used in most situations when someone is complaining, moaning, etc. It might be your boss complaining that your report is late - *"That must have been awkward not having it for the meeting. I'm sorry about that. Is there anything I can do now to help?"*

It could be that one of your children is moaning that you forgot to remind them at two o'clock to take their medication (and the time is only ten to two). *"You seem really annoyed that I didn't remind you. I'm sorry you are annoyed. What time did you want to be reminded?"*

"At two o'clock!"

"And what's the time now?"

Almost always, when an angry person is complaining in a Defend/Attack style and the response they receive is calm and empathic, the complainer changes his or her tune. They usually end up apologising for the way they approached the situation.

These steps are logical and easy to follow. When a Customer Service Director attended one of our Interpersonal Skills training workshops, he noted that the Complaint Handling Module only took about fifteen minutes to facilitate, and asked me if I would train all his customer service staff in these simple steps.

I had to point out to him that the first step, 'Listen to Understand', was everything we had covered in the workshop to that point, which had taken almost one-and-a-half days. Step one is the most difficult step because one's instinct in facing situations such as complaints is to justify and defend. To listen with the intention of understanding might take a minute or even ten minutes depending upon the situation and the circumstances. And step two, 'Respond with Empathy', cannot be accomplished unless you have been listening with empathy.

Summary

Always be aware of your intention. Do you want to maintain the relationship? Do you want to help the person who is complaining? If you do, you now have a clear and effective strategy for handling any kind of complaint.

*   Listen to understand.
*   Empathise (*feeling* and *about what*).
*   Apologise (*without accepting or placing the blame elsewhere*).
*   Take action to rectify the situation (*first find out what the other person wants*).

Always within the context of:

*   Enhancing, or at least maintaining, the self-esteem of others.
*   Listening and responding with empathy.
*   Involving others.

"Statistics suggest that when customers complain, business owners and managers ought to get excited about it. The complaining customer represents a huge opportunity for more business."

Zig Ziglar

One of the reasons we laugh at comedy sketches is that, even though they may be ridiculously far-fetched, somehow they are still true to life. Take for example, one of my favourite complaint-handling scenes, *Monty Python's famous Parrot Sketch* featuring John Cleese as Mr Praline and Michael Palin as the shop owner:

A customer enters a pet shop.

Mr Praline: *'Ello, I wish to register a complaint.*

(The owner does not respond.)

Mr Praline: *'Ello, Miss?*

Owner: *What do you mean 'Miss'?*

Mr Praline: (pause) *I'm sorry, I have a cold. I wish to make a complaint!*

Owner: *We're closin' for lunch.*

Mr Praline: *Never mind that, my lad. I wish to complain about this parrot what I purchased not half an hour ago from this very boutique.*

Owner: *Oh yes, the, uh, the Norwegian Blue. What's, uh, what's wrong with it?*

Mr Praline: *I'll tell you what's wrong with it, my lad. 'E's dead, that's what's wrong with it!*

Owner: *No, no, 'e's uh, ...he's resting.*

Mr Praline: *Look, matey, I know a dead parrot when I see one and I'm looking at one right now.*

Owner: *No, no, he's not dead, he's, he's restin'! Remarkable bird, the Norwegian Blue, idn'it, ay? Beautiful plumage!*

Mr Praline: *The plumage don't enter into it. It's stone dead.*

Owner: *Nononono, no, no! 'E's resting.*

Mr Praline: *All right then, if he's restin', I'll wake him up!* (Shouting at the cage). *'Ello, Mister Polly Parrot! I've got a lovely fresh cuttle fish for you if you show...*

(Owner hits the cage)

Owner: *There, he moved!*

Mr Praline: *No, he didn't, that was you hitting the cage!*

Owner: *I never!!*

Mr Praline: *Yes, you did!*

Owner: *I never, never did anything...*

Mr Praline: (Yelling and hitting the cage repeatedly) *'ELLO POLLY!! Testing! Testing! Testing! Testing! This is your nine o'clock alarm call!*

(Takes parrot out of the cage and thumps its head on the counter. Throws it up in the air and watches it plummet to the floor.)

Mr Praline: *Now that's what I call a dead parrot.*

We have all come across people like this. Someone who denies responsibility, argues with the complainer, blames others, etc. I hope not to the extreme of the Parrot Sketch but sometimes it seems pretty close.

Application

I hope for your sake that you don't receive any complaints very soon but, realistically, everyone encounters some kind of moan or complaint sooner or later. That is the time to apply the four steps.

The first step, *Listen to Understand*, is usually the difficult one as it requires patience and listening from the other person's point of view. But, if you do that effectively, you will find steps two, three and four very quick, easy and effective.

*"Your most unhappy customers
are your greatest source of learning."*

Bill Gates

Connection Exercise

Notebook Exercise: Connecting

This is an exercise to help you reflect on how the communication skills described in the previous chapters can help you to get on with the people that you might consider very difficult.

1. Think back to a few instances when you didn't connect with someone as well as you would have liked to, or as well as you could have done.

2. List what it was that prevented you from really connecting with that person, or what it was that made it more difficult for you to do so. Make a note of this *before reading any further*.

3. When you have completed that, note down three things you could have done that would have increased the effectiveness of the interaction, created comfortable rapport, and generally improved the communication process.

4. Now consider the single most important insight that you have learned from completing this exercise, and how you are going to put it into action. Take a look at the guidelines on the next page to ensure that action takes place.

"You are what you do,
not what you say you'll do."

C. G. Jung

Taking Action

"Action may not always bring happiness,
but there is no happiness without action."

Benjamin Disraeli

Now it is time to put your insight into action. List a specific action you will take that describes:

*   What you will actually be doing.
*   How you will be doing it.
*   When you will be doing it.
*   When you will have completed it.
*   How you will know when you have been successful.

And do it!

"You can't build a reputation
on what you are going to do."

Henry Ford

"The secret of getting ahead is getting started.
The secret of getting started is breaking your complex
overwhelming tasks into small manageable tasks,
and then starting on the first one."

Mark Twain

"Action will remove the doubts
that theory cannot solve."

Tehyi Hsieh

Managers:
Delivering Difficult Messages

The problem won't go away by ignoring it

Managers: Delivering Difficult Messages

The purpose of these discussions is to improve behaviour, not to punish it.

Handling difficult conversations is one of the more challenging parts of a manager's role. It is relatively easy to deliver a difficult message and leave a person feeling de-motivated, but it takes skill, gravitas, and diplomacy to deliver it whilst maintaining self-esteem and motivation.

If your intention is to support the individual and/or improve performance, you can use the following structure to deliver your message effectively.

1. **Set the agenda - *What and Why*.**
2. **Ask for their input.**
3. **Listen to understand.**
4. **Make expectations clear.**
5. **Close the loop / Discuss the next steps.**

1. Set the Agenda - *What* and *Why*

It is most important to set a clear focus for the conversation right up-front. Far too often, managers focus only on generalisations such as a person's attitude, or on a measure of performance. Focusing on targets and numbers is an important part of a manager's role and gives a valuable indication of the *effect* of a person's behaviour. But the correct way to start this type of conversation is to address a specific behaviour - something the person has said or done that you feel needs improving.

Open the discussion by briefly and simply stating *'What'* (*the observable behaviour*) you want to speak to them about and *'Why'* you want to speak to them about it. This sets the agenda and the tone for the meeting right from the outset. For example:

"I'd like to talk to you about some of the remarks you made about customers in the team meeting yesterday, because I was concerned about the impression you made on some of the new people."

2. Ask For Their Input

It is important that you ask them to explain their point of view or reasons for their behaviour before taking the discussion any further. For example:

"Could you tell me why this happened?" or, *"I'd like to understand your point of view on this."*

3. Listen to Understand

It is pointless asking them for their input if you are not going to listen to it. Listening with the *intention* of understanding their perceptions, motivation, etc., will provide you with the substance you need to take the discussion further (or not).

4. Make Expectations Clear

The purpose of these discussions is to improve behaviour rather than to punish it. Make your expectations *crystal clear* at this stage and check that they fully understand the *specific behaviour* that is required of them in the future.

Most of the time we assume that expectations are crystal clear because, to us, they seem to be common sense. But just because it is crystal clear to you doesn't mean it is to anyone else. The easiest way to check if your expectations are clear is to ask yourself, *"If someone else asked that person what they think I expected them to do in a certain situation, what would they say? What would their actual words be?"* If you have any doubts as to what their answer might be, then your expectations are not crystal clear.

5. Close the Loop / Discuss the Next Steps

Depending upon the situation and the circumstances, the action you take in this step can vary considerably. Sometimes no further action is necessary other than the need for you to reinforce their improved behaviour with appropriate feedback at a later stage. It might be necessary to schedule a follow-up meeting or to make them aware of the consequences that will follow if their behaviour does not change to the required standards.

Summary

Make sure that your intention is to improve performance rather than punish it, and then conduct the conversation using the following steps:

1. Set the agenda - *What* you want to speak to them about and *Why* you want to speak to them about it.
2. Ask for their input.
3. Listen to understand.
4. Make expectations clear.
5. Close the loop / Discuss the next steps.

Application

- Make a list of those difficult conversations that you have been avoiding.

- Prepare for the discussion by scripting the conversation using the structure outlined in this chapter.

- If appropriate, ask a colleague or friend to role-play the conversation with you to provide practice and feedback.

- Schedule the conversations to take place as soon as possible. The quicker an issue or behaviour is addressed, the easier it is to have the conversation. Not having the conversation can be perceived as condoning the behaviour.

Final Summary

Enhance, or at least maintain, the self-esteem of others.
Listen and respond with empathy.
Involve others.

The Three Key Principles

"The first principle of value that we need to rediscover is this: that all reality hinges on moral foundations. In other words, that this is a moral universe and that there are moral laws of the universe just as abiding as the physical laws."

Martin Luther King Jr.

I have no doubt that, if you have been applying the behaviours outlined in this book, you will have already made a significant positive impact on your relationships. All the content of this book is centred on the Three Key Principles so if you ever want to measure your effectiveness in any interpersonal situation, check yourself against the following:

Enhance, or at least maintain, the self-esteem of others

"Our prime purpose in this life is to help others. And if you can't help them, at least don't hurt them."

Dalai Lama

We all want to feel valued; be heard; be seen; be included; be involved; be respected; be listened to; be understood; and be loved. We all want to feel important. Everyone has an inherent need to feel valued and appreciated and, if you provide this acknowledgment specifically and sincerely, you are laying down the foundations for a solid relationship.

Listen and respond with empathy

"The most basic of all human needs is the need to understand and be understood. The best way to understand people is to listen to them."

Ralph G. Nichols

Empathy is not about how *you* would feel. It is about trying to understand how the other person is feeling. You can't respond with empathy unless you have been listening with empathy. In other words, you first need to try and understand how they are feeling before you can respond. Instead of saying, *"I understand how you feel, it happened to me too,"* simply consider how you think they are feeling and check it out. For example: *"You seem to be quite worried about how it is affecting your relationship?"*

Involve others

The principle of involving others also meets the natural need people have of wanting to feel important. The more you genuinely involve others, the more they will feel important, and the more likely they will be to buy into the discussion or the required actions.

Interpersonal Skills
Customised Training Workshops

The challenge in writing this book was to do so in a style that met most of the common learning preferences. It was, however, not intended as a replacement for a training workshop. In an interactive workshop, people have the opportunity to question, challenge, discuss, and get involved in skill-practice exercises. All this helps to facilitate behavioural change.

And what good is training unless it results in a positive change in individual behaviour? In order to ensure behavioural change, we offer a free and no-obligation Behavioural Needs Analysis (in the United Kingdom and South Africa). This will help you assess current behaviour and its specific cause, clarify desired behaviours, and then determine whether training or coaching will provide you with an appropriate solution and a return on your investment.

Russ Baleson Training will customise programmes specifically for your company. All content is tailored and continuously adjusted to meet both the company's objectives and each delegate's specific personal needs.

 The People and Management Training Specialists
http://russbalesontraining.co.uk